Title: "Divine Systems: The Ch1 Entrepreneurship"

The ultimate goal of life is not to remain perpetually working. Hard work, in itself, can be seen as counterproductive. The Bible states, *"He who does not work must not eat,"* suggesting that work is necessary for sustenance but not for wealth creation. Relying solely on income from work leads to poverty.

God's example during the creation illustrates this principle. He worked for six days, but His concept of work involved creating systems that function independently. For instance, God created trees as a self-sustaining system. The seed of the tree produces another tree, which bears fruits containing more seeds. These seeds fall, rot, and grow into new trees. God does not need to recreate trees continually. The system operates autonomously.

Similarly, the sun and moon are systems that God set in motion. The sun rotates, and thousands of years after creation, it continues to function without direct intervention. The same applies to the moon.

To emulate God's method, one must establish systems that generate income without constant personal involvement. A job can be a starting point, but it should not be the end goal. A job is beneficial if it provides the means to develop a business or system that eventually operates independently of your presence.

Even in business, the focus should be on creating systems. The objective is to manage these systems rather than being constantly involved in their operation. Just as God created systems and then appointed Adam to manage them, we should aim to create self-sustaining systems that require minimal direct oversight.

God's rest after creation exemplifies the efficiency of systems. He did not concern Himself with the minutiae of how many trees there were. Instead, He entrusted Adam to manage the system. God's interactions with Adam were straightforward: checking if everything was functioning smoothly.

Thus, the essence of sustainable success lies in establishing efficient, self-sustaining systems. This approach not only brings rest but also aligns with the divine method of creation and management.

Preface

In an age where the business world is ever-evolving, driven by rapid technological advancements and shifting market dynamics, the quest for sustainable success and enduring legacy becomes even more critical. As an entrepreneur and educator, I have witnessed firsthand the challenges and triumphs faced by those who venture into the world of business. This book, "Entrepreneurship by Design: Building Wealth and Legacy with Biblical Principles," is born out of a desire to merge the timeless wisdom of Scripture with the practical demands of modern entrepreneurship.

Throughout my career, I have been privileged to work with students and professionals from diverse backgrounds, guiding them as they navigate the complexities of economics, business management, and entrepreneurship. My extensive teaching experience across different cultures and countries has provided me with a unique perspective on the universal principles that underpin successful enterprises. It is this perspective that I bring to you in this book.

The Bible is not just a spiritual guide but also a rich source of practical wisdom that can be applied to every aspect of life, including business. By examining the Scriptures, we can uncover profound insights into work, wealth creation, stewardship, and legacy building. This book aims to demonstrate how biblical principles can serve as a solid foundation for entrepreneurial ventures, providing both ethical guidance and strategic direction.

Each chapter of this book delves into a specific aspect of entrepreneurship, drawing parallels between biblical teachings and contemporary business practices. From understanding the divine mandate for work to creating self-sustaining systems, from leveraging God-given talents to balancing faith with business risks, this book offers a comprehensive roadmap for entrepreneurs seeking to align their business endeavors with their faith.

As you read through these pages, I encourage you to reflect on the scriptural references and consider how they apply to your own entrepreneurial journey. My hope is that this book will not only provide you with practical tools and strategies but also inspire you to pursue your business goals with integrity, wisdom, and a deep sense of purpose.

Ultimately, true success in entrepreneurship is not merely about financial gain but about building something that honors God, benefits others, and leaves a lasting impact. May this book guide you towards that noble pursuit.

With gratitude and blessings,

Prologue

The intersection of faith and entrepreneurship is a terrain less traveled, yet it holds immense potential for those willing to explore it. As I embarked on my journey in the world of business and academia, I realized the profound impact that biblical principles could have on entrepreneurial ventures. This realization inspired me to write "Entrepreneurship by Design: Building Wealth and Legacy with Biblical Principles."

In the fast-paced, competitive realm of business, many seek quick success and immediate gratification. However, the Bible offers a different perspective—one that emphasizes diligence, wisdom, and long-term vision. It teaches us that true prosperity is not just about accumulating wealth but about creating value, serving others, and building a legacy that endures through generations.

My own experiences have reinforced the importance of integrating faith into every aspect of life, including business. I have seen how biblical principles can provide clarity and direction, guiding entrepreneurs through the uncertainties and challenges of the business world. These principles are timeless, offering a blueprint for success that transcends cultural and economic boundaries.

In writing this book, I drew upon my diverse background in entrepreneurship, economics, and business management, as well as my extensive teaching and research experience. Each chapter is crafted to offer practical insights and actionable strategies, all rooted in the rich soil of biblical wisdom. The goal is not only to help you succeed in your entrepreneurial endeavors but also to encourage you to build businesses that reflect the values of integrity, stewardship, and service.

The journey of entrepreneurship is filled with highs and lows, risks and rewards. It requires a blend of innovation, resilience, and strategic thinking. Yet, above all, it requires faith—faith in your vision, faith in your abilities, and most importantly, faith in God's provision and guidance.

As you begin this book, I invite you to open your heart and mind to the lessons contained within. Let the Scriptures inspire you, let the practical advice equip you, and let the stories of faith and entrepreneurship encourage you. Whether you are a seasoned entrepreneur or just starting out, my hope is that this book will be a source of inspiration, guidance, and blessing on your journey.

May you find wisdom in these pages and may your entrepreneurial endeavors be fruitful, honoring God and benefiting others.

Contents

- Preface 3
- Prologue 5
- Chapter 1: Christian entrepreneurship 7
- Chapter 2: God's Creation Model: Systems in Action 11
- Chapter 3: Emulating God's Efficiency 16
- Chapter 4: The Power of Systems in Business 21
- Chapter 5: Financial Wisdom from the Scriptures 27
- Chapter 6: Leveraging God-Given Talents 32
- Chapter 7: Faith and Risk in Entrepreneurship 38
- Chapter 8: Building a Legacy 43
- Conclusion: Rest in God's Provision 48

Chapter 1: Christian entrepreneurship

Introduction

The essence of Christian entrepreneurship is grounded in biblical principles and the example set by God during creation. This book explores the law of systems and how it aligns with the teachings of the Bible to guide believers towards establishing self-sustaining ventures. By leveraging divine wisdom, Christians can build enterprises that not only provide for their needs but also serve the greater good.

The Divine Mandate for Work

From the beginning of creation, work has been integral to human existence. In Genesis, we see God assigning Adam the task of tending to the Garden of Eden:

"The Lord God took the man and put him in the Garden of Eden to work it and take care of it." (Genesis 2:15, NIV)

This scripture establishes the first principle of work: it is ordained by God. Adam's responsibility in the garden was not a punishment but a purposeful engagement designed to care for God's creation. This divine assignment underscores the dignity and significance of work in God's eyes.

Paul's admonition in 2 Thessalonians 3:10 reiterates this principle. His stern instruction to the Thessalonians emphasizes that work is essential for survival: *"The one who is unwilling to work shall not eat."* This directive was meant to address idleness and to remind the early

Christians that everyone must contribute to their sustenance.

Work as a Means, Not an End

While the Bible mandates work, it also presents a nuanced view that distinguishes between working for sustenance and creating lasting wealth. The key is understanding that work is a means to an end, not the end itself. Proverbs 14:23 states, *"All hard work brings a profit, but mere talk leads only to poverty."* This verse highlights that diligent labor is necessary and beneficial, but it should be paired with wisdom and planning.

Consider the story of Joseph in Genesis 41. Joseph's administrative skills and foresight enabled Egypt to prepare for seven years of famine. His work wasn't just about daily survival; it was strategic, designed to ensure long-term prosperity for the entire nation. Joseph's story exemplifies how work, combined with divine wisdom and planning, can lead to sustainable success.

The Dangers of Idleness

The Bible also warns against idleness and the dangers it poses. In Proverbs 6:6-11, Solomon uses the ant as an example of diligence and foresight:

"Go to the ant, you sluggard; consider its ways and be wise! It has no commander, no overseer or ruler, yet it stores its provisions in summer and gathers its food at harvest. How long will you lie there, you sluggard? When will you get up from your sleep? A little sleep, a little slumber, a little folding of the hands to rest—and poverty will

come on you like a thief and scarcity like an armed man."

This passage reinforces the importance of proactive, diligent work and the consequences of laziness. It teaches that while rest is important, it must not devolve into neglect of responsibilities.

Work and Wisdom: Building Lasting Prosperity

Proverbs 24:27 advises, *"Put your outdoor work in order and get your fields ready; after that, build your house."* This scripture encapsulates the principle of planning and preparation. It suggests that before establishing permanent structures (symbolic of long-term investments or business ventures), one must ensure that their immediate work and responsibilities are in order.

Jesus Himself taught about the importance of wise planning in Luke 14:28-30: *"Suppose one of you wants to build a tower. Won't you first sit down and estimate the cost to see if you have enough money to complete it? For if you lay the foundation and are not able to finish it, everyone who sees it will ridicule you, saying, 'This person began to build and wasn't able to finish.'"*

These verses highlight the importance of strategic thinking and planning in any endeavor. Work should not be aimless; it must be directed towards clear, sustainable goals.

The Role of Faith in Work

While the Bible emphasizes diligent work, it also underscores the necessity of faith. Proverbs 16:3 encourages, *"Commit to the Lord whatever you do, and he will establish your plans."* Faith in

God provides the foundation and direction for our work. It ensures that our efforts align with His will and purpose, leading to true success.

The balance of work and faith is beautifully illustrated in Psalm 127:1-2: *"Unless the Lord builds the house, the builders labor in vain. Unless the Lord watches over the city, the guards stand watch in vain. In vain you rise early and stay up late, toiling for food to eat—for he grants sleep to those he loves."*

This passage reminds us that while work is essential, it must be grounded in faith and dependence on God. Our efforts are futile without His blessing and guidance.

Conclusion

The biblical foundation of work teaches us that work is a divine mandate necessary for sustenance and fulfilling God's purpose. However, it also emphasizes that work should be paired with wisdom, planning, and faith to create lasting prosperity. As Christians, we are called to work diligently, avoid idleness, and trust in God's guidance to build enterprises that not only meet our needs but also reflect His glory and purpose. By understanding and applying these principles, we can embark on a path of entrepreneurship that is both fruitful and fulfilling, aligned with the divine blueprint for our lives.

Chapter 2: God's Creation Model: Systems in Action

Scriptural Reference: *"By the seventh day God had finished the work he had been doing; so on the seventh day he rested from all his work."* *(Genesis 2:2, NIV)*

God's creation narrative is the perfect illustration of systems in action. For six days, God worked to create a self-sustaining world. Trees, for example, were designed to reproduce without continuous intervention. This chapter explores how these natural systems can inspire entrepreneurial ventures that operate efficiently and autonomously.

The Six Days of Creation: A Blueprint for Systems

God's methodical approach to creation over six days provides a detailed blueprint for establishing systems. Each day, He introduced components of the universe that interdependently support and sustain life. This meticulous process highlights the importance of planning, structuring, and sequencing in creating functional systems.

1. **Day 1 - Light and Darkness**: God separated light from darkness, establishing a fundamental cycle that governs time and seasons. For entrepreneurs, this illustrates the importance of creating order and predictability within their businesses.

2. **Day 2 - Sky and Water**: By separating the waters, God created the sky, ensuring a balance between atmospheric conditions and aquatic systems. This act emphasizes the need for balance and harmony in business operations.

3. **Day 3 - Land, Sea, and Vegetation**: God gathered the waters to reveal dry land and created vegetation that reproduces through seeds. This showcases the importance of foundational structures and renewable resources in sustaining business growth.

4. **Day 4 - Sun, Moon, and Stars**: God established celestial bodies to govern time, seasons, and years. This underlines the significance of long-term planning and strategic foresight in entrepreneurial ventures.

5. **Day 5 - Marine and Avian Life**: The creation of creatures in the sea and birds in the air introduced dynamic systems of life that interact and thrive. For businesses, this highlights the need for diversity and adaptability within their systems.

6. **Day 6 - Land Animals and Humans**: The creation of animals and humans, with humans given the task to manage and steward the earth, underscores the role of leadership and stewardship in maintaining and enhancing systems.

The Principle of Self-Sustaining Systems

One of the most striking aspects of God's creation is the principle of self-sustainability. Trees, for instance, are designed to reproduce without continuous divine intervention. A tree produces fruit, which contains seeds. These seeds fall to the ground, germinate, and grow into new trees. This cyclical process ensures the perpetuation of the species without external input.

For entrepreneurs, this principle is invaluable. Businesses should be designed to function autonomously, generating value and sustaining themselves with minimal direct oversight. This involves creating robust processes, developing reliable products or services, and fostering a culture of continuous improvement and innovation.

Case Study: Nature's Systems

Examining natural systems can provide profound insights into creating effective business systems. Consider the water cycle: it involves evaporation, condensation, precipitation, and collection. This cycle is a closed-loop system that maintains balance and sustainability.

Similarly, a well-designed business system should include the following elements:

1. **Input**: Resources such as capital, raw materials, and labor.

2. **Process**: Conversion of inputs into products or services through efficient workflows.

3. **Output**: Finished products or services delivered to customers.

4. **Feedback**: Customer feedback and market data used to refine and improve processes.

By modeling business processes on natural systems, entrepreneurs can create operations that are efficient, adaptable, and resilient.

Implementing God's Model in Business

To implement God's creation model in business, entrepreneurs can follow these steps:

1. **Vision and Planning**: Just as God had a vision for creation, entrepreneurs must have a clear vision and strategic plan for their businesses. This includes defining goals, identifying resources, and outlining processes.

2. **Structuring Systems**: Establishing clear structures and roles within the business ensures that every aspect functions cohesively. This involves setting up departments, defining workflows, and creating standard operating procedures.

3. **Automation and Delegation**: Leveraging technology and delegating tasks to capable individuals can help create self-sustaining systems. Automation tools can handle repetitive tasks, while a skilled team can manage operations efficiently.

4. **Continuous Improvement**: Just as natural systems adapt and evolve, businesses must embrace a culture of continuous improvement. This involves regularly reviewing processes,

seeking feedback, and making necessary adjustments.

5. **Sustainability**: Like the self-replicating nature of trees, businesses should focus on sustainability. This includes not only financial sustainability but also environmental and social responsibility.

Practical Examples

1. **Franchising**: McDonald's is an example of a business that operates on a well-defined system. Each franchise operates independently, following standardized processes that ensure consistent quality and efficiency.

2. **Software as a Service (SaaS)**: Companies like Salesforce provide software platforms that users can access and utilize independently. These platforms are designed to be scalable and self-

sustaining, with regular updates and customer support integrated into the system.

3. **E-commerce Automation**: Amazon employs advanced automation in its warehouses, utilizing robots and sophisticated logistics to manage inventory and fulfill orders with minimal human intervention.

Conclusion

God's creation model offers profound insights into the power of systems. By designing the world to operate autonomously, God set a precedent for efficiency, sustainability, and continuous operation. Entrepreneurs can draw inspiration from this model to build businesses that are not only profitable but also sustainable and resilient. By focusing on creating self-sustaining systems, leveraging automation, and embracing continuous improvement, entrepreneurs can ensure their ventures thrive independently, reflecting the divine wisdom embedded in creation.

Chapter 3: Emulating God's Efficiency

Scriptural Reference: *"Then the Lord God took the man and put him in the Garden of Eden to work it and take care of it." (Genesis 2:15, NIV)*

After creating the world, God appointed Adam to manage it. This chapter highlights the importance of management and stewardship in entrepreneurship. It explains how entrepreneurs can create and oversee systems that thrive independently, mirroring the efficiency of God's creation.

The Role of Adam: A Model for Stewardship

In Genesis 2:15, God places Adam in the Garden of Eden to *"work it and take care of it."* This act of entrusting Adam with the garden underscores the importance of stewardship. Adam's role was to maintain and oversee the systems God had put in place, ensuring their continuous and efficient operation.

For entrepreneurs, this biblical example serves as a model for effective management. It highlights the necessity of:

1. **Responsibility**: Taking ownership of the business and its processes.

2. **Oversight**: Regularly monitoring and maintaining business systems.

3. **Sustainability**: Ensuring the long-term health and productivity of the enterprise.

Key Principles of Effective Stewardship

1. **Vision and Purpose**: Just as Adam was given a clear purpose in the garden, entrepreneurs must have a clear vision and purpose for their businesses. This vision acts as a guiding star,

ensuring all efforts align with the overall mission.

2. **Resource Management**: Effective stewardship involves the prudent management of resources. This includes financial resources, human capital, and physical assets. Entrepreneurs should ensure that resources are used efficiently and sustainably.

3. **Delegation and Empowerment**: God entrusted Adam with the responsibility of the garden, demonstrating the importance of delegation. Entrepreneurs should empower their teams, delegating tasks and responsibilities to capable individuals to ensure smooth operation and innovation.

4. **Continuous Improvement**: Stewardship requires a commitment to continuous

improvement. Entrepreneurs should regularly assess business processes, seek feedback, and implement improvements to enhance efficiency and productivity.

5. **Accountability**: Stewards are accountable for their actions. Entrepreneurs must establish systems of accountability within their businesses, ensuring that everyone is responsible for their roles and contributions.

Creating Self-Sustaining Systems

To emulate God's efficiency, entrepreneurs need to create self-sustaining systems. These systems should be designed to operate independently, minimizing the need for constant oversight. Here are steps to achieve this:

1. **Standardization**: Develop standardized processes and procedures that ensure

consistency and quality across all operations. This includes creating manuals, checklists, and training programs.

2. **Automation**: Leverage technology to automate repetitive tasks and processes. Automation not only increases efficiency but also reduces the risk of human error.

3. **Scalability**: Design systems that can scale with the growth of the business. This involves creating flexible processes that can adapt to increased demand without compromising on quality or efficiency.

4. **Redundancy**: Implement redundancy within critical systems to ensure continuity in case of failures. This could include backup systems, cross-training employees, and diversifying suppliers.

5. **Monitoring and Evaluation**: Establish robust monitoring and evaluation mechanisms to track the performance of business systems. Use key performance indicators (KPIs) and regular audits to ensure systems are functioning as intended.

Case Study: Effective Stewardship in Action

Consider the example of Toyota, a company renowned for its efficient management systems. The Toyota Production System (TPS) is a prime example of how effective stewardship and management principles can create a self-sustaining system.

1. **Lean Manufacturing**: TPS emphasizes lean manufacturing, focusing on eliminating waste and optimizing processes. This mirrors the biblical principle of prudent resource management.

2. **Continuous Improvement (Kaizen)**: Toyota's commitment to continuous improvement, known as Kaizen, ensures that all processes are regularly reviewed and enhanced. This aligns with the principle of continuous improvement in stewardship.

3. **Employee Empowerment**: Toyota empowers its employees, encouraging them to take ownership of their roles and contribute to process improvements. This reflects the biblical principle of delegation and empowerment.

By applying these principles, Toyota has created a system that is efficient, sustainable, and capable of thriving independently.

Practical Steps for Entrepreneurs

1. **Define Your Vision and Mission**: Clearly articulate the vision and mission of your

business. Ensure that all team members understand and align with these guiding principles.

2. **Develop Standard Operating Procedures (SOPs)**: Create detailed SOPs for all critical processes. Ensure that these procedures are documented and easily accessible to all team members.

3. **Invest in Technology**: Identify areas where technology can enhance efficiency and invest in appropriate tools and systems. This could include automation software, customer relationship management (CRM) systems, and inventory management solutions.

4. **Train and Empower Your Team**: Provide regular training and development opportunities for your team. Encourage a culture of ownership

and accountability, where team members are empowered to take initiative and contribute to continuous improvement.

5. **Implement Monitoring Systems**: Establish systems to monitor and evaluate the performance of your business processes. Use data and analytics to identify areas for improvement and make informed decisions.

Conclusion

Emulating God's efficiency in entrepreneurship involves creating and overseeing systems that operate independently and sustainably. By applying principles of effective stewardship, such as vision, resource management, delegation, continuous improvement, and accountability, entrepreneurs can build businesses that reflect the divine efficiency of God's creation. Through diligent management and a commitment to excellence, entrepreneurs can ensure their ventures thrive, fulfilling their purpose and glorifying God in the process.

Chapter 4: The Power of Systems in Business

Scriptural Reference: *"Go to the ant, you sluggard; consider its ways and be wise! It has no commander, no overseer or ruler, yet it stores its provisions in summer and gathers its food at harvest." (Proverbs 6:6-8, NIV)*

This chapter examines the concept of systems in business. Drawing parallels with the ant's self-sufficient behavior, it underscores the importance of creating businesses that can operate without constant oversight, ensuring sustainability and growth.

The Wisdom of the Ant

Proverbs 6:6-8 invites us to learn from the ant, a creature that exemplifies self-sufficiency and diligence. The ant operates without a commander, overseer, or ruler, yet it efficiently gathers and stores food, ensuring its survival and prosperity.

Key lessons from the ant include:

1. **Self-Motivation**: Ants work diligently without needing external supervision.

2. **Preparation**: They gather food in times of plenty to prepare for periods of scarcity.

3. **Teamwork**: Ants collaborate effectively, contributing to the colony's overall success.

These principles are directly applicable to business. Entrepreneurs can create systems that promote self-motivation, preparation, and teamwork to ensure sustainability and growth.

The Importance of Business Systems

Business systems are the structured procedures and processes that guide the day-to-day operations of a company. Effective systems enable a business to run smoothly, efficiently, and independently of constant oversight. Here are some reasons why business systems are crucial:

1. **Consistency**: Systems ensure that tasks are performed consistently, maintaining quality and reliability.

2. **Efficiency**: Streamlined processes reduce waste and improve productivity.

3. **Scalability**: Well-defined systems can be scaled up as the business grows.

4. **Resilience**: Systems provide a framework that can withstand changes and challenges.

Creating Self-Sufficient Business Systems

To create self-sufficient business systems, entrepreneurs should focus on several key areas:

1. **Standard Operating Procedures (SOPs)**: Documenting SOPs for all critical tasks ensures that employees can perform their duties consistently and correctly. This includes procedures for production, customer service, finance, and more.

2. **Automation**: Leveraging technology to automate repetitive tasks can significantly enhance efficiency. Automation tools can handle tasks such as invoicing, inventory management, and customer relationship management.

3. **Training and Development**: Investing in employee training ensures that staff are competent and capable of performing their roles

without constant supervision. Continuous development opportunities help employees stay updated with industry best practices.

4. **Decentralized Decision-Making**: Empowering employees to make decisions within their scope of work fosters a culture of responsibility and initiative. This decentralization can lead to faster problem-solving and innovation.

5. **Feedback Loops**: Establishing feedback mechanisms allows for continuous improvement. Regularly soliciting feedback from customers and employees can help identify areas for enhancement and streamline operations.

Case Study: The Ant's Efficiency in Business

Consider a company like Starbucks, which exemplifies the principles seen in the ant's behaviour:

1. **Self-Motivation**: Starbucks encourages a culture of ownership among its employees, known as "partners." This self-motivation drives employees to deliver excellent customer service consistently.

2. **Preparation**: Starbucks meticulously plans its inventory, supply chain, and seasonal promotions. This preparation ensures that they can meet customer demands efficiently, regardless of the season.

3. **Teamwork**: Starbucks' success relies heavily on teamwork. Baristas, managers, and corporate staff work collaboratively to ensure a seamless customer experience.

Through these systems, Starbucks operates efficiently, ensuring sustainability and growth, even with minimal direct oversight from top management.

Practical Steps to Implement Systems in Your Business

1. **Identify Key Processes**: Determine which processes are critical to your business operations. These could include customer service, production, sales, and finance.

2. **Document Procedures**: Create detailed documentation for each key process. This documentation should include step-by-step instructions, checklists, and any relevant forms or templates.

3. **Automate Where Possible**: Identify tasks that can be automated and invest in appropriate technology solutions. Automation can save time and reduce the risk of errors.

4. **Train Your Team**: Provide comprehensive training for your employees on the documented procedures and the use of automation tools. Ensure they understand their roles and responsibilities.

5. **Establish Monitoring Systems**: Implement systems to monitor the performance of your processes. Use key performance indicators (KPIs) and regular audits to ensure that your systems are functioning as intended.

6. **Solicit Feedback**: Encourage feedback from employees and customers to identify areas for improvement. Use this feedback to refine and enhance your systems continuously.

Conclusion

The ant's wisdom, as highlighted in Proverbs 6:6-8, teaches us the importance of self-sufficiency, preparation, and teamwork. By creating robust business systems that operate independently, entrepreneurs can ensure sustainability and growth. These systems not only enhance efficiency and consistency but also empower employees and foster a culture of continuous improvement. By emulating the ant's behaviour, business leaders can build resilient enterprises that thrive without constant oversight, reflecting the wisdom embedded in God's creation.

Chapter 5: Financial Wisdom from the Scriptures

Scriptural Reference: *"The plans of the diligent lead to profit as surely as haste leads to poverty."* (Proverbs 21:5, NIV)

Financial literacy is crucial for entrepreneurs. This chapter provides biblical insights on financial management, planning, and investment. It emphasizes the need for prudent financial practices to build and sustain successful enterprises.

The Importance of Financial Planning

Proverbs 21:5 highlights the significance of diligent planning in achieving profit. Financial planning is not merely about budgeting and saving but involves strategic forecasting, risk management, and investment. Entrepreneurs must adopt a holistic approach to financial planning to ensure long-term sustainability and growth.

Key Aspects of Financial Planning:

1. **Budgeting**: Creating a detailed budget helps in tracking income and expenses, ensuring that resources are allocated efficiently.

2. **Forecasting**: Projecting future financial performance based on historical data and market trends allows for better decision-making.

3. **Risk Management**: Identifying potential financial risks and developing strategies to mitigate them safeguards the business against unforeseen challenges.

4. **Investment**: Allocating resources to growth opportunities can enhance profitability and business expansion.

Biblical Principles of Financial Management

1. **Diligence and Prudence**: As Proverbs 21:5 suggests, diligent planning leads to profit. Entrepreneurs should be meticulous in their financial planning and cautious in their spending and investments.

2. **Avoiding Debt**: Proverbs 22:7 warns that *"the borrower is slave to the lender."* While some debt can be necessary for business growth, it should be managed carefully to avoid financial bondage.

3. **Generosity and Giving**: Luke 6:38 teaches that generosity leads to blessings. Entrepreneurs should incorporate giving into their financial

practices, supporting charitable causes and reinvesting in their communities.

4. **Savings and Investments**: Proverbs 13:11 states, *"Dishonest money dwindles away, but whoever gathers money little by little makes it grow."* Consistent saving and wise investments are crucial for financial stability and growth.

Practical Financial Strategies for Entrepreneurs

1. **Create a Comprehensive Budget**: Outline all sources of income and categorize expenses. Regularly review and adjust the budget to reflect changes in business operations and market conditions.

2. **Build an Emergency Fund**: Set aside a portion of profits to create an emergency fund. This fund

acts as a financial cushion during periods of low revenue or unexpected expenses.

3. **Invest in Growth**: Identify areas where investment can yield significant returns. This could include expanding product lines, entering new markets, or adopting new technologies.

4. **Monitor Cash Flow**: Keep a close eye on cash flow to ensure that the business remains solvent. Implement measures to improve cash flow, such as optimizing inventory levels and accelerating receivables.

5. **Seek Professional Advice**: Consult with financial advisors or accountants to gain expert insights and develop robust financial strategies.

Case Study: Joseph's Financial Wisdom

The story of Joseph in Genesis 41 provides a compelling example of financial wisdom and planning. Joseph interpreted Pharaoh's dream, predicting seven years of abundance followed by seven years of famine. He advised storing surplus grain during the years of plenty to prepare for the coming scarcity.

Joseph's strategy involved:

1. **Resource Management**: Efficiently gathering and storing surplus grain during the prosperous years.

2. **Strategic Planning**: Forecasting future needs based on prophetic insight and preparing accordingly.

3. **Crisis Management**: Successfully navigating the years of famine by utilizing the stored resources.

Entrepreneurs can learn from Joseph's example by adopting proactive and strategic financial planning, ensuring their businesses can withstand economic fluctuations.

The Role of Integrity in Financial Practices

Integrity is a fundamental biblical principle that should underpin all financial practices. Proverbs 11:1 state, *"The Lord detests dishonest scales, but accurate weights find favour with him."* Honest and transparent financial dealings build trust with stakeholders, including customers, employees, and investors.

Practices for Maintaining Financial Integrity:

1. **Accurate Record-Keeping**: Maintain precise and up-to-date financial records. Use reliable accounting software and conduct regular audits.

2. **Transparent Reporting**: Provide clear and honest financial reports to stakeholders. Transparency fosters trust and credibility.

3. **Ethical Decision-Making**: Make financial decisions based on ethical considerations, ensuring fairness and justice in all transactions.

Practical Steps for Implementing Financial Wisdom

1. **Develop a Financial Plan**: Create a detailed financial plan that includes budgeting, forecasting, and investment strategies. Review and update the plan regularly.

2. **Educate Yourself**: Invest time in learning about financial management principles and practices. Attend workshops, read relevant books, and seek mentorship.

3. **Adopt Financial Tools**: Utilize financial management tools and software to streamline processes and enhance accuracy.

4. **Practice Generosity**: Allocate a portion of profits to charitable giving. This practice not only aligns with biblical principles but also fosters goodwill and community support.

5. **Evaluate Investments**: Carefully assess potential investments to ensure they align with your business goals and values. Diversify investments to spread risk.

Conclusion

Financial wisdom from the Scriptures provides a solid foundation for entrepreneurial success. By adopting biblical principles of diligence, prudence, integrity, and generosity, entrepreneurs can build and sustain thriving businesses. Through careful planning, strategic investments, and ethical practices, they can navigate financial challenges and achieve long-term prosperity, reflecting the wisdom and stewardship God desires for His people.

Chapter 6: Leveraging God-Given Talents

Scriptural Reference: *"Each of you should use whatever gift you have received to serve others, as faithful stewards of God's grace in its various forms." (1 Peter 4:10, NIV)*

God has endowed each person with unique talents and abilities. This chapter encourages readers to identify and leverage their God-given talents to create businesses that not only generate income but also serve the community and glorify God.

Understanding Your God-Given Talents

Every person possesses distinctive skills and talents, often aligned with their passions and interests. Identifying these talents is the first step toward using them effectively in business.

Steps to Identify Your Talents:

1. **Self-Reflection**: Take time to reflect on your interests, strengths, and the activities that bring you joy and fulfilment.

2. **Seek Feedback**: Ask friends, family, and colleagues for their observations about your strengths and talents.

3. **Experiment and Explore**: Try different activities and roles to discover what resonates with you and where you excel.

4. **Prayer and Meditation**: Seek God's guidance through prayer and meditation, asking Him to reveal your unique gifts and how you can use them to serve His purposes.

Biblical Examples of Leveraging Talents

The Bible provides numerous examples of individuals who used their talents to serve God and others:

1. **Joseph**: Joseph's gift of interpreting dreams and his administrative skills led him to become a key figure in Egypt, ultimately saving many lives during a famine (Genesis 41).

2. **Bezalel and Oholiab**: These artisans were endowed with skills in craftsmanship and were chosen to design and construct the Tabernacle (Exodus 31:1-11).

3. **Paul**: The Apostle Paul used his abilities in teaching, writing, and tent-making to spread the Gospel and support himself (Acts 18:3, 1 Corinthians 9:14-15).

These examples demonstrate that God-given talents, when used faithfully, can have a significant impact on both individual lives and broader communities.

Building a Business Around Your Talents

Creating a business that leverages your talents involves aligning your skills with market needs and opportunities. Here are steps to build such a business:

1. **Identify Market Needs**: Research and identify gaps in the market where your talents can provide unique solutions. Understand the problems your potential customers face and how your skills can address them.

2. **Develop a Unique Value Proposition**: Clearly articulate what sets your business apart from competitors. Highlight how your unique talents and skills translate into exceptional value for your customers.

3. **Create a Business Plan**: Develop a comprehensive business plan that outlines your goals, target market, marketing strategies, financial projections, and operational plans.

4. **Seek Mentorship and Support**: Surround yourself with mentors and advisors who can provide guidance, support, and insights. Their experience can help you navigate challenges and capitalize on opportunities.

5. **Invest in Continuous Learning**: Stay updated with industry trends, enhance your skills, and adapt to changes. Continuous learning ensures that your business remains competitive and relevant.

Serving Others Through Your Business

1 Peter 4:10 emphasizes using our gifts to serve others as faithful stewards of God's grace.

Entrepreneurs can incorporate this principle by focusing on how their businesses can benefit others.

Ways to Serve Others Through Your Business:

1. **Quality Products and Services**: Ensure that your offerings genuinely meet customer needs and improve their lives.

2. **Community Involvement**: Engage with your community by supporting local initiatives, creating job opportunities, and contributing to social causes.

3. **Ethical Practices**: Operate your business with integrity, fairness, and transparency. Treat employees, customers, and partners with respect and dignity.

4. **Charitable Giving**: Allocate a portion of your profits to charitable organizations or causes that align with your values and mission.

5. **Education and Empowerment**: Use your platform to educate and empower others, sharing knowledge and resources that can help them succeed.

Case Study: Leveraging Talents for Business and Community Impact

Consider the example of Dave Ramsey, a well-known financial advisor and entrepreneur. Ramsey leveraged his talent for financial management and communication to build a successful business that provides financial education and counselling. His company, Ramsey Solutions, offers resources, courses, and programs designed to help individuals and families achieve financial peace.

Key Elements of Ramsey's Success:

1. **Identifying a Need**: Recognizing the widespread issue of financial mismanagement and debt, Ramsey used his skills to address these problems.

2. **Providing Value**: His offerings provide practical, actionable advice that genuinely helps people improve their financial situations.

3. **Serving the Community**: Ramsey Solutions actively supports charitable initiatives and provides free resources to those in need.

4. **Faithful Stewardship**: Ramsey incorporates his Christian faith into his business, emphasizing

principles of stewardship, integrity, and generosity.

Practical Steps for Entrepreneurs

1. **Conduct a Talent Audit**: List your skills, experiences, and passions. Identify how they can be applied to create value in the marketplace.

2. **Align Talents with Business Goals**: Ensure that your business goals align with your talents and passions. This alignment increases motivation and the likelihood of success.

3. **Develop a Service Mindset**: Approach your business with a mindset of service. Consider how your talents can best serve your customers and community.

4. **Create a Mission Statement**: Craft a mission statement that reflects your commitment to

leveraging your talents for the glory of God and the benefit of others.

5. **Measure Impact**: Regularly evaluate the impact of your business on your customers, employees, and community. Use this feedback to refine and enhance your offerings.

Conclusion

Leveraging God-given talents in business is a powerful way to fulfil your purpose, serve others, and glorify God. By identifying your unique gifts and aligning them with market needs, you can create a business that not only generates income but also makes a meaningful impact. Embrace the wisdom of 1 Peter 4:10, using your talents as faithful stewards of God's grace, and witness the transformative power of entrepreneurship grounded in faith and service.

Chapter 7: Faith and Risk in Entrepreneurship

Scriptural Reference: *"Trust in the Lord with all your heart and lean not on your own understanding; in all your ways submit to him, and he will make your paths straight." (Proverbs 3:5-6, NIV)*

Entrepreneurship involves risk, but with faith in God, these risks can be managed wisely. This chapter discusses how Christian entrepreneurs can balance faith and business risks, trusting in God's guidance and provision.

Understanding Risk in Entrepreneurship

Risk is an unavoidable element of entrepreneurship. It involves stepping into the unknown, making decisions with incomplete information, and investing resources without guaranteed returns. Successful entrepreneurs are those who can manage and mitigate these risks effectively.

Types of Risks in Entrepreneurship:

1. **Financial Risk**: The potential loss of money invested in the business.

2. **Market Risk**: Uncertainty regarding market acceptance and customer demand.

3. **Operational Risk**: Risks associated with the day-to-day operations of the business.

4. **Strategic Risk**: Risks related to business decisions and long-term strategies.

The Role of Faith in Managing Risk

Proverbs 3:5-6 calls us to trust in the Lord wholeheartedly and not rely solely on our understanding. This scripture emphasizes the importance of submitting our plans and decisions to God, trusting that He will guide us on the right path.

Faith as a Risk Management Tool:

1. **Divine Guidance**: Faith in God ensures that we seek His guidance in every decision. Prayer and meditation help align our plans with God's will.

2. **Peace of Mind**: Trusting in God's provision and sovereignty provides peace, reducing the anxiety associated with risk.

3. **Wisdom and Discernment**: God grants wisdom to those who seek it (James 1:5). This wisdom aids in making informed and prudent decisions.

4. **Community Support**: Faith communities offer support, advice, and resources, helping entrepreneurs navigate challenges.

Biblical Examples of Faith and Risk

The Bible is replete with stories of individuals who took significant risks based on their faith in God:

1. **Noah**: Noah built the ark based on God's instruction, facing ridicule and uncertainty. His

faith in God's plan saved humanity and animal life (Genesis 6-9).

2. **Abraham**: Abraham left his homeland for an unknown destination, trusting God's promise of a great nation. His faith was rewarded with God's covenant (Genesis 12).

3. **Esther**: Queen Esther risked her life by approaching the king to save her people. Her faith and courage led to the deliverance of the Jews (Esther 4-7).

These examples show that taking risks in alignment with God's direction can lead to significant outcomes and blessings.

Balancing Faith and Practical Risk Management

While faith is crucial, practical risk management strategies are also essential. Entrepreneurs must balance their trust in God with practical steps to mitigate risks.

Practical Risk Management Strategies:

1. **Research and Planning**: Conduct thorough market research and develop detailed business plans. Understanding the market landscape and potential challenges is key to managing risks.

2. **Diversification**: Avoid putting all resources into a single venture or strategy. Diversifying investments and income streams can reduce overall risk.

3. **Financial Prudence**: Manage finances wisely. Maintain a healthy cash flow, avoid excessive debt, and build an emergency fund.

4. **Insurance**: Consider appropriate insurance policies to protect against unforeseen events and liabilities.

5. **Legal Compliance**: Ensure that the business complies with all legal and regulatory requirements. This reduces the risk of legal issues that can disrupt operations.

6. **Adaptability**: Be prepared to pivot and adapt to changing circumstances. Flexibility in strategy and operations can help navigate unexpected challenges.

Case Study: Faith and Risk in Modern Entrepreneurship

Consider the example of Truett Cathy, the founder of Chick-fil-A. Cathy's faith played a pivotal role in his business decisions, including the risk of closing all Chick-fil-A restaurants on

Sundays to honor the Sabbath. This decision, rooted in faith, seemed risky in the fast-food industry. However, it exemplified Cathy's trust in God's provision.

Key Elements of Cathy's Approach:

1. **Faith-Driven Decisions**: Cathy's decision to close on Sundays was based on his belief in honoring God, demonstrating trust over financial gain.

2. **Customer Loyalty**: This act of faith resonated with many customers who appreciated the company's values, fostering loyalty.

3. **Business Success**: Despite initial skepticism, Chick-fil-A became one of the most successful fast-food chains, illustrating how faith and principles can coexist with business success.

Practical Steps for Entrepreneurs

1. **Submit Plans to God**: Regularly pray and seek God's guidance for your business decisions. Trust that He will direct your paths.

2. **Incorporate Faith in Business Practices**: Let your faith guide your business ethics and decisions. Honesty, integrity, and service should be at the forefront of your operations.

3. **Develop a Risk Management Plan**: Identify potential risks and create strategies to mitigate them. Regularly review and update this plan.

4. **Build a Support Network**: Engage with a community of fellow believers who can offer support, prayer, and practical advice.

5. **Stay Flexible**: Be open to God's leading and willing to adjust your plans as needed. Flexibility

allows you to respond to changing circumstances effectively.

Conclusion

Faith and risk are integral aspects of entrepreneurship. By trusting in God and seeking His guidance, Christian entrepreneurs can navigate the uncertainties of business with confidence and peace. Balancing faith with practical risk management strategies ensures that businesses not only survive but thrive, reflecting God's wisdom and provision. Embrace the call of Proverbs 3:5-6, trusting in the Lord with all your heart, and watch as He makes your entrepreneurial paths straight.

Chapter 8: Building a Legacy

Scriptural Reference: *"A good person leaves an inheritance for their children's children, but a sinner's wealth is stored up for the righteous."* *(Proverbs 13:22, NIV)*

True success in entrepreneurship is not just about immediate gains but about building a lasting legacy. This chapter explores how to create enduring wealth and businesses that can be passed down through generations, in alignment with biblical principles.

Understanding Legacy in a Biblical Context

Proverbs 13:22 highlights the importance of leaving an inheritance not just for one's children but for their children's children. This scripture underscores the value of long-term thinking and planning in wealth creation.

Components of a Biblical Legacy:

1. **Spiritual Values**: Passing down faith and moral principles.

2. **Financial Stability**: Creating wealth that sustains and supports future generations.

3. **Reputation and Integrity**: Building a name that is respected and honored.

4. **Knowledge and Wisdom**: Sharing insights and experiences to guide future generations.

Building Enduring Wealth

Creating wealth that lasts involves strategic planning, wise investments, and a focus on sustainability. Here are key steps to build enduring wealth:

1. **Long-Term Financial Planning**: Develop a financial plan that includes savings,

investments, and retirement planning. Ensure it aligns with long-term goals.

2. **Diversification**: Spread investments across different asset classes to mitigate risks and enhance growth potential.

3. **Estate Planning**: Prepare for the future by creating a will, setting up trusts, and planning for the transfer of wealth in a tax-efficient manner.

4. **Education and Mentorship**: Equip future generations with the financial knowledge and skills they need to manage and grow the inheritance.

Biblical Principles for Creating Lasting Businesses

1. **Integrity and Honesty**: Proverbs 10:9 states, "Whoever walks in integrity walks securely, but whoever takes crooked paths will be found out." Building a business on a foundation of integrity ensures long-term trust and respect.

2. **Diligence and Hard Work**: Proverbs 12:24 says, "Diligent hands will rule, but laziness ends in forced labor." Consistent effort and dedication are crucial for sustained success.

3. **Generosity and Stewardship**: Proverbs 11:25 emphasizes, "A generous person will prosper; whoever refreshes others will be refreshed." Practicing generosity and responsible stewardship of resources fosters goodwill and divine favor.

4. **Innovation and Adaptability**: Proverbs 16:3 advises, "Commit to the Lord whatever you do,

and he will establish your plans." Seeking God's guidance in innovation and being adaptable to change are essential for longevity.

Case Study: The Legacy of the Green Family

The Green family, founders of Hobby Lobby, exemplify the principles of building a legacy. David Green started Hobby Lobby with a $600 loan, and today it is one of the largest arts and crafts retailers in the world. The family's commitment to Christian values, generous giving, and ethical business practices has ensured their legacy.

Key Elements of the Green Family's Legacy:

1. **Faith-Based Principles**: The Greens run their business according to biblical principles, closing on Sundays to honor the Sabbath and treating employees with respect and fairness.

2. **Generosity**: They are known for their philanthropic efforts, giving generously to Christian ministries and educational institutions.

3. **Succession Planning**: The family has implemented a succession plan, ensuring that future generations are prepared to lead the business.

4. **Community Impact**: Through their business and philanthropic efforts, the Greens have made a significant positive impact on their community and beyond.

Practical Steps for Entrepreneurs

1. **Develop a Succession Plan**: Identify and train successors to ensure a smooth transition and continuity of leadership. Consider both family members and key employees.

2. **Instill Values in Future Generations**: Teach children and heirs the importance of faith, integrity, and hard work. Encourage them to uphold these values in their personal and professional lives.

3. **Create a Legacy Statement**: Write a statement outlining the vision and values you want to pass down. This document can guide future generations in maintaining the legacy.

4. **Invest in Relationships**: Build strong relationships with family, employees, and the community. These connections are vital for sustaining a lasting legacy.

5. **Focus on Sustainability**: Implement sustainable practices in your business to ensure it can thrive for generations. This includes environmental stewardship, ethical sourcing, and long-term financial planning.

The Role of Generosity in Legacy Building

Generosity is a key biblical principle that enhances legacy building. By giving back to the community and supporting charitable causes, entrepreneurs can create a positive and lasting impact.

Ways to Practice Generosity:

1. **Tithing and Donations**: Regularly give a portion of your income to your church and charitable organizations.

2. **Community Projects**: Invest in community development projects that improve the quality of life for others.

3. **Employee Welfare**: Ensure fair wages, good working conditions, and opportunities for growth for your employees.

4. **Mentorship**: Offer mentorship and support to aspiring entrepreneurs and young professionals.

Conclusion

Building a legacy involves more than accumulating wealth; it's about creating a lasting impact through faith, values, and generosity. By aligning entrepreneurial efforts with biblical principles, Christian entrepreneurs can ensure that their businesses and wealth benefit future generations, honoring God and leaving a meaningful inheritance. Embrace the wisdom of

Proverbs 13:22, aiming to leave a legacy that reflects God's grace and provision, influencing the world positively for years to come

Conclusion: Rest in God's Provision

Scriptural Reference: "Come to me, all you who are weary and burdened, and I will give you rest." (Matthew 11:28, NIV)

The journey of entrepreneurship can be challenging, but God promises rest for those who trust in Him. The conclusion reinforces the importance of faith, rest, and reliance on God's provision, encouraging readers to pursue their entrepreneurial dreams with divine wisdom and peace.

The Promise of Rest

In Matthew 11:28, Jesus extends an invitation to those who are weary and burdened, promising rest to those who come to Him. This promise is not merely a call for physical rest but a deep, soul-refreshing peace that transcends the pressures of life and work.

Key Aspects of Rest in God's Provision:

1. **Spiritual Peace**: True rest comes from trusting in God's sovereignty and letting go of anxiety about the future. It's an acknowledgment that, despite our efforts, the ultimate outcome is in God's hands.

2. **Emotional Relief**: Entrepreneurship can be emotionally taxing, filled with stress and uncertainty. Rest in God provides comfort and reassurance, alleviating emotional burdens.

3. **Renewal and Strength**: Rest in God replenishes our strength and energy, enabling us to face challenges with renewed vigor and perspective.

4. **Divine Guidance**: Trusting in God's provision involves seeking His guidance in every decision, ensuring that our plans align with His will and purpose.

The Role of Faith in Finding Rest

Faith in God is foundational to finding rest. It means believing in His promises, surrendering our worries, and relying on His provision.

Practical Ways to Cultivate Faith and Rest:

1. **Daily Prayer and Meditation**: Establish a routine of daily prayer and meditation to seek God's presence and guidance. This practice helps center your focus on Him rather than on the pressures of business.

2. **Scripture Reading**: Regularly read and meditate on scriptures that reinforce God's promises and

provision. Verses like Philippians 4:6-7 and Isaiah 41:10 offer comfort and encouragement.

3. **Surrender Control**: Acknowledge that while you can control your efforts and decisions, the ultimate results are in God's hands. Surrender your plans and worries to Him.

4. **Rest in the Sabbath**: Follow the example of resting on the Sabbath as a day of physical and spiritual renewal. This practice helps maintain balance and perspective in your work.

5. **Seek Community Support**: Engage with a supportive faith community. Share your burdens and seek prayer and encouragement from others who understand the entrepreneurial journey.

Balancing Work and Rest

While faith in God's provision offers rest, it's also important to balance work with periods of rest and rejuvenation. This balance is essential for sustained productivity and well-being.

Strategies for Balancing Work and Rest:

1. **Set Boundaries**: Establish clear boundaries between work and personal time. Avoid letting work consume all your time and energy.

2. **Prioritize Self-Care**: Regularly engage in activities that refresh and rejuvenate you, whether it's exercise, hobbies, or spending time with loved ones.

3. **Delegate and Collaborate**: Share responsibilities with others and seek help when needed. Delegating tasks and collaborating with others can alleviate workload and stress.

4. **Evaluate Workload**: Periodically assess your workload and make adjustments as needed to prevent burnout and maintain a healthy work-life balance.

Embracing God's Provision in Entrepreneurship

Incorporating faith into entrepreneurship involves recognizing that God is the ultimate provider and guide. Embracing His provision means approaching your business with a spirit of gratitude and trust.

Ways to Embrace God's Provision:

1. **Acknowledge God's Role**: Recognize and give thanks for the ways God has provided and guided you in your entrepreneurial journey. Share testimonies of His provision with others.

2. **Practice Contentment**: Cultivate a heart of contentment with what you have, trusting that God will provide what you need in His timing.

3. **Act with Integrity**: Conduct your business with integrity, reflecting your faith in all dealings. Trust that God honors those who honor Him through their work.

4. **Celebrate Successes and Learn from Failures**: Celebrate milestones and achievements as signs of God's favor. Learn from setbacks with the understanding that they are opportunities for growth and reliance on Him.

Conclusion

The journey of entrepreneurship is indeed challenging, but the promise of rest in God's provision offers profound solace and assurance. By trusting in His guidance, surrendering our anxieties, and embracing His promises, we can approach our entrepreneurial endeavors with a sense of peace and confidence. As you move forward in your business, remember the invitation of Matthew 11:28: come to God with your burdens, and He will give you rest. Let this promise guide and sustain you, allowing your faith to be the foundation upon which you build your entrepreneurial dreams.

Printed in Great Britain
by Amazon